God only sends us sadness

and the agony of sorrow

To help our ever-restless souls

grow to meet tomorrow . . .

Presented to

GILL

(& MY MUM!) } ABOVE

from (& PEPPER!) .

PHIL, ROSALIE, ROBIN & SMOKIE — BELOW .

Books in the Just Because Series
Moments of Celebration
Moments of Comfort
Moments of Friendship
Moments of Love

Other beloved books by Helen Steiner Rice
A New Beginning
An Instrument of Your Peace
An Old-Time Christmas
Blossoms of Friendship
Celebrations of the Heart
For Each New Day
Gifts of Love
God's Promises from A to Z
Inspiration for Living
Loving Promises
Lovingly: Poems for All Seasons
Mother, I Love You
Somebody Loves You
Someone Cares
To Mother with Love

THE
Just Because
SERIES

Moments of Comfort

HELEN STEINER RICE

Fleming H. Revell
A Division of Baker Book House Co
Grand Rapids, Michigan 49516

© 2002 by Virginia Ruehlmann
and The Helen Steiner Rice Foundation

Published by Fleming H. Revell
a division of Baker Book House Company
P.O. Box 6287, Grand Rapids, MI 49516-6287

Poems taken from *A Book of Comfort* by Helen Steiner Rice, compiled by Virginia J. Ruehlmann, published
in 1994. Biographical information drawn from *Helen Steiner Rice: Ambassador of Sunshine* by Ronald Pollitt
and Virginia Wiltse, published in 1994.

Printed in the United States of America

Library of Congress Cataloging-in-Publication Data is on file at the Library of Congress, Washington, D.C.

ISBN 0-8007-1798-8

Unless otherwise indicated, Scripture quotations are taken from the Revised Standard Version of the Bible,
copyright 1946, 1952, 1971 by the Division of Christian Education of the National Council of the
Churches of Christ in the USA. Used by permission.

Scripture marked NIV is taken from the HOLY BIBLE, NEW INTERNATIONAL VERSION®. NIV®.
Copyright © 1973, 1978, 1984 by International Bible Society. Used by permission of Zondervan Publish-
ing House. All rights reserved.

Cover and interior design by Robin Black

For current information about all releases from Baker Book House, visit our web site:
http://www.bakerbooks.com

Comfort, Moment by Moment

Are You Broken in Heart?

Helen Steiner Rice would understand. She lost her loved ones and her dreams; suffered financial reverses and unjust accusations; endured loneliness, depression, disability, and infirmity. Her poetry sprang from personal heartaches and her attempts to heal and learn from them.

Her search for meaning led her into the mystery of God's love. Along the way, she realized she'd become a wounded healer—a woman who, because she honestly attended her own wounds, was able to transform her sorrow into a source of healing for others. This became her greatest joy.

What worked for Helen can work for you. She will tell you that in the poetry that follows. Read between the lines. Look, as Helen did, beyond what seem like broken fragments of life and you'll find something wholly new. Your life is like a kaleidoscope right now. Watch and listen, in the silence or the clamor, as things shift and change. Give yourself time. Focus on beauty and truth. Moments of comfort will come to you. Take them. Moment by moment you can know what Helen learned and penned: "The agony of sorrow . . . [helps] our ever-restless souls grow to meet tomorrow." There, in the pile of things broken, is something surprisingly stronger and more beautiful.

Losses

Are yours many? Isn't even one enough? Helen's came in waves: Her beloved father unexpectedly died in the flu epidemic of 1918. Because she was just out of high school and her family needed a breadwinner, Helen gave up her dream of college and went to work. Her hope of a law career faded with the realities of earning a living. She stayed in business.

Her marriage in January 1929 to a young bank trust officer and vice president was not to mark the beginning of a long and happy relationship. The stock market crashed in October of that year, and her husband's bank closed in December. Their debts mounted. Jobless for almost three years, Helen's despairing husband drove their car into the garage, his final letter to Helen in his coat pocket, and breathed in the carbon monoxide. Helen was 32. Life as she'd known it shattered. But Helen gave herself time to turn over the pieces. Here is what she found.

Whenever I am troubled

and lost in deep despair,
I bundle all my troubles up
and go to God in prayer.
I tell Him I am heartsick
and lost and lonely, too,
That my mind is deeply burdened
and I don't know what to do.
But I know He stilled the tempest
and calmed the angry sea,
And I humbly ask if, in His love,
He'll do the same for me.
And then I just keep quiet
and think only thoughts of peace,
And as I abide in stillness
my restless murmurings cease.

"Life is eternal," the good Lord said,
    so do not think of your loved one as dead,
For death is only a stepping-stone
    to a beautiful life we have never known,
A place where God promised us we would be
    eternally happy and safe and free,
A wonderful land where we live anew
    when our journey on earth is over and through.
So trust God and doubt Him never,
    for all who love Him live forever,
And while we cannot understand
    just let the Savior take your hand,
For when death's angel comes to call
    God is so great and we're so small.
And there is nothing you need to fear,
    for faith in God makes all things clear.

Death is a gateway
 we all must pass through
To reach the fair land
 where the soul's born anew,
For we're born to die,
 and our sojourn on earth
Is a short span of years
 beginning with birth.
And like pilgrims we wander
 until death takes our hand,
And we start on the journey
 to God's Promised Land—
A place where we'll find
 no suffering or tears,
Where time is not counted
 in days, months, or years.
And in that fair city
 that God has prepared
Are unending joys
 to be happily shared
With all our loved ones
 who patiently wait
On death's other side
 to open the gate.

Let not your hearts be troubled; believe in God, believe also in me. In my Father's house are many rooms; if it were not so, would I have told you that I go to prepare a place for you? And when I go and prepare a place for you, I will come again and will take you to myself, that where I am you may be also.

JOHN 14:1–3

When I must leave you for a little while
    please do not grieve and shed wild tears
And hug your sorrow to you through the years,
    but start out bravely with a smile.
And for my sake and in my name
    live on and do all the things the same.
Feed not your loneliness on empty days
    but fill each waking hour in useful ways.
Reach out your hand in comfort and in cheer,
    and I, in turn, will comfort you and hold you near.
And never, never be afraid to die,
    for I am waiting for you in the sky.

The Master Gardener
from heaven above
Planted a seed
in the garden of love,
And from it there grew
a rosebud small
That never had time
to open at all.
For God in His perfect
and all-wise way
Chose this rose
for His heavenly bouquet,
And great was the joy
of this tiny rose
To be the one our Father chose
to leave earth's garden
For one on high
where roses bloom always
And never die.

So while you can't see
    your precious rose bloom
You know the great Gardener
    from the upper room
Is watching and tending
    this wee rose with care,
Tenderly touching
    each petal so fair.
So think of your darling
    with the angels above,
Secure and contented
    and surrounded by love,
And remember God blessed
    and enriched your lives, too,
For in dying your darling
    brought heaven closer to you.

Peace I leave with you; my peace I give to you; not as the world gives do I give to you. Let not your hearts be troubled, neither let them be afraid.

JOHN 14:27

On the wings
   of death and sorrow
God sends us
   new hope for tomorrow,
And in His mercy
   and His grace
He gives us strength
   to bravely face
The lonely days
   that stretch ahead
And know our loved one
   is not dead
But only sleeping
   and out of sight
Until we meet in that land
   that is always bright.

What fills the empty places or eases the pangs left by loss? After her husband's suicide, Helen wondered too. She sorted through the reminders of the past, giving away things that didn't matter (clothes, old shoes) and keeping what did (a letter, some photographs, memories). She worked and traveled, and she befriended others whom she sensed were trying to navigate life, if not better understand it.

Helen spent many hours in introspection, where she penned her personal ten commandments, including "Thou shalt always do thy best and leave the rest to God." Still, a question haunted her: Was love—of people, of dreams—worth the price it exacted? Her poetry and favorite Scriptures, chronicled in this quest and reflected in her life's work, give answer.

There are many things in life
that we cannot understand
But we must trust God's judgment
and be guided by His hand,
And all who have God's blessings
can rest safely in His care,
For He promises safe passage
on the wings of faith and prayer.

And behold, there arose a
great storm on the sea,
so that the boat was being
swamped by the waves; but
he was asleep. And then they
went and woke him, saying,
"Save Lord; we are perishing."
And he said to them, "Why
are you afraid, O men of little
faith?" Then he rose and
rebuked the winds and the sea;
and there was a great calm.
And the men marveled, saying,
"What sort of man is this, that
even winds and sea obey him?"

MATTHEW 8:24–27

There is always hope of tomorrow
    to brighten the clouds of today.
There is always a corner for turning,
    no matter how weary the way.
So just look ahead to tomorrow
    and trust that you'll find waiting there
The sunlight that seemed to be hidden
    by yesterday's clouds of despair.

In this restless world of struggle
    it is very hard to find
Answers to the questions
    that daily come to mind.
We cannot see the future,
    what's beyond is still unknown,
For the secret of God's kingdom
    still belongs to Him alone.
But He granted us salvation
    when His Son was crucified,
For life became immortal
    because our Savior died.

If we did not go to sleep at night,
　　we'd never awaken to see the light,
And the joy of watching a new day break
　　or meeting the dawn by some quiet lake
Would never be ours unless we slept
　　while God and all His angels kept
A vigil through this little death
　　that's over with the morning's breath.
And death, too, is a time of sleeping,
　　for those who die are in God's keeping,
And there's sunrise for each soul,
　　for life, not death, is God's promised goal.

Jesus said to her, "I am the resurrection and the life; he who believes in me, though he die, yet shall he live, and whoever lives and believes in me shall never die. Do you believe this?"

JOHN 11:25–26

Truth, Comfort

What is left once you've counted your losses? Helen returned to this question throughout life, especially in October, on the anniversaries of her father's and husband's deaths. She routinely fell into depression, followed by more pronounced loneliness. Her journals, letters, and poetry often refer to her dark night of the soul. Always she came back to the same conclusion, tempered by time: "All that was beyond my understanding then, now I see as part of God's plan. . . . Before Franklin died I was a piece of fluff—there was nothing to my life—it was all fun, and I mean I was counting for nothing. The death of Franklin is what God used to make me a person of substance, and to do things for His benefit and not my own. . . . I was not familiar with the earth before I arrived here. The Creator got me safely here, and so He will take me safely back without me knowing the full particulars."

Do not fear,

for I am with you;

do not be dismayed,

for I am your God.

Isaiah 41:10 (NIV)

There is no night without a dawning,
no winter without a spring,
And beyond death's dark horizon
our hearts once more will sing.
For those who leave us for a while
have only gone away
Out of a restless, careworn world
into a brighter day
Where there will be no partings
and time is not counted by years,
Where there are no trials or troubles,
no worries, no cares, and no tears.

I will turn their mourning into gladness;
I will give them comfort and joy
instead of sorrow.

JEREMIAH 31:13 (NIV)

Just close your eyes
and open your heart
And feel your worries
and cares depart.
Yield yourself
to the Father above
And let Him hold you
secure in His love.
For He hears every prayer
and answers each one
When we pray in His name,
"Thy will be done,"
And the burdens that seemed
too heavy to bear
Are lifted away
on the wings of prayer.

Although it sometimes seems to us
    our prayers have not been heard,
God always knows our every need
    without a single word.
And He will not forsake us
    even though the way seems steep,
For always He is near to us,
    a tender watch to keep.
And in good time He'll answer us,
    and in His love He'll send
Greater things than we have asked
    and blessings without end.
So though we do not understand
    why trouble comes to man,
Can we not be contented
    just to know that it's God's plan?

What more can we ask of our Father
than to know we are never alone,
That His mercy and love are unfailing,
And He makes all our problems His own.

The eternal God is your

dwelling place, and underneath

are the everlasting arms.

DEUTERONOMY 33:27

The Lord is our salvation
 and our strength in every fight,
Our Redeemer and Protector
 our eternal guiding light.
He has promised to sustain us,
 He's our refuge from all harms,
And He holds us all securely
 in His everlasting arms!

All who believe in God's mercy and grace
Will meet their loved ones face to face
Where time is endless and joy unbroken
And only the words of God's love are spoken.

Death is a season that all must pass through
and, just like the flowers, God wakens us, too.
So why should we grieve when our loved ones die?
We'll meet them again in a cloudless sky.

Something Stronger,
More Beautiful

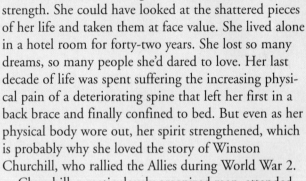

Faith in what cannot be seen gave Helen Steiner Rice strength. She could have looked at the shattered pieces of her life and taken them at face value. She lived alone in a hotel room for forty-two years. She lost so many dreams, so many people she'd dared to love. Her last decade of life was spent suffering the increasing physical pain of a deteriorating spine that left her first in a back brace and finally confined to bed. But even as her physical body wore out, her spirit strengthened, which is probably why she loved the story of Winston Churchill, who rallied the Allies during World War 2.

Churchill, a meticulously organized man, attended to all details in his life—even his funeral, planned well ahead of its occurrence. Favorite Scripture, beloved hymns, preferred readings were described and itemized. Upon his death, his instructions were followed precisely. But funeral attendees sat astonished when the service concluded with not just one bugler, stationed high in the dome of St. Paul's Cathedral, but a second. The first played the traditional taps. Across the dome, however, and in perfect counterpoint, the second bugler played reveille. The message was never lost on Helen: Get up. Begin a new day.

May you find comfort in the thought
that sorrow, grief, and woe
Are sent into our lives sometimes
to help our souls to grow.
For through the depths of sorrow
comes understanding love,
And peace and truth and comfort
are sent from God above.

Flowers sleeping 'neath the snow,
    awakening when the spring winds blow;
Leafless trees so bare before,
    gowned in lacy green once more;
Hard, unyielding, frozen sod
    now softly carpeted by God;
Still streams melting in the spring,
    rippling over rocks that sing;
Barren, windswept, lonely hills
    turning gold with daffodils.
These miracles are all around
    within our sight and touch and sound,
As true and wonderful today
    as when the stone was rolled away
Proclaiming to all women and men
    that in God all things live again.

After the winter comes the spring
    to show us again that in everything
There's always a renewal divinely planned,
    flawlessly perfect, the work of God's hand.
And just like the seasons that come and go
    when the flowers of spring lay buried in snow,
God sends to the heart in its winter of sadness
    a springtime awakening of new hope and gladness,
And loved ones who sleep in a season of death
    will, too, be awakened by God's life-giving breath.

May tender memories
    soften your grief,
May fond recollection
    bring you relief,
And may you find comfort
    and peace in the thought
Of the joy that knowing
    your loved one brought.
For time and space
    can never divide
Or keep your loved one
    from your side
When memory paints
    in colors true
The happy hours
    that belonged to you.

And I heard a loud voice from the throne saying,

"Behold, the dwelling of God is with men.

He will dwell with them, and they shall be his people,

and God himself will be with them; he will wipe every tear

from their eyes, death shall be no more, neither shall

there be mourning nor crying nor pain any more,

for the former things have passed away."

REVELATION 21:3–4

When death brings weeping
    and the heart is filled with sorrow,
It calls us to seek God
    as we ask about tomorrow.
And in these hours of heart-hurt,
    we draw closer to believing
That even death, in God's hands,
    is not a time for grieving
But a time for joy in knowing
    death is just a stepping-stone
To a life that's everlasting,
    such as we have never known.

Whatever the celebration, whatever the day, whatever the event or occasion, Helen Steiner Rice possessed the ability to express the appropriate feeling for that particular moment. A happening became happier, a sentiment more sentimental, a memory more memorable because of her deep sensitivity and ability to put into understandable language the emotion being experienced. Her positive attitude, concern for others, and love of God are identifiable threads woven into her life, work, and even her death.

Just before her passing, she established the Helen Steiner Rice Foundation. Because of limited resources, the Foundation presently limits grants to qualified charitable programs in Lorain, Ohio, where she lived and worked most of her life. It is the Foundation's hope that in the future resources will be of sufficient size that broader geographical areas may be considered in the awarding of grants.

Because of her foresight, caring, and deep conviction of sharing, Helen Steiner Rice continues to touch a countless number of lives through Foundation grants and through her inspirational poetry.

Thank you for your help to keep Helen's dream alive and growing.

ANDREA E. CORNETT, ADMINISTRATOR
THE HELEN STEINER RICE FOUNDATION